72 Messages of Love

Jason Rotman

DEDICATIONS

My wife - Pia Rotman: Pia, your love and support of everything I do is amazing and priceless. You are the best and I love you so much. You are my soulmate and you are so beautiful!

My children - Makale'a, Solana, and Solomon: You fill my life with pure joy. I am so incredibly grateful for every moment I get to spend with you. I love you.

My late father - Jesse Rotman: Dad, I miss you. I hope you love this book and I know you are watching over my family with love. Thank you for visiting me in my dreams. Your spirit of creativity has deeply inspired me.

My mother - Diana Rotman: Mom, you are simply the best Mom. Your unconditional, unwavering love has nourished me at the deepest level and I am forever grateful for you.

My sister - Betsy Ross: Betsy, you are amazing and thank you for being a fun, inspiring, and wise sister. I love how compassionate and purpose-driven of a person you are.

To you, the reader - I dedicate this book to deepening your sense of love, joy, gratitude, and beauty.

CONTENTS

Introduction

Here is how you can get a simple, easy, and daily serving of love, beauty, and inspiration in your life without looking for it in a million different places...

Read 72 Messages of Love!

I created this book of messages to provide a spark of Divine remembrance to your soul.

These 72 Messages of Love will help you get deeply centered in a mindset of love, gratitude, and joy everyday.

Reading this book will help you affirm your highest calling and live your most inspired life.

I hope you love the original poems and affirmations, as well as the carefully selected quotes from various wonderful and inspirational people throughout history.

Thank you and enjoy 72 Messages of Love,
Jason

Yes, Really

The faces change
the smiles sparkle on
love is the energy
keeps the world spinning 'round
listen to the call
listen to the healing
your heart is your guide
a living breathing being
meditational breath
devotional feelings
have an inner knowing
that there is no ceiling
yes, really

"Have the courage to follow your heart and intuition."

– Steve Jobs

My intuition guides all of my choices today

The Value of Love

The value of love
is more than we can measure
it's a grace, a beauty
a bliss, a bellwether
we don't always see
how glorious life is
we're just so used to it
so here's a pop quiz:
who do you love?
why are you here?
what can you let go of?
let your illusions disappear
the value of love
is more than we can measure
it's a peace, a promise
a joy, a treasure

"The truth is that existence wants your life to become
a festival."

– Osho

Love is my highest priority today

Messages in Bottles

We walk upright
and sleep horizontal
angular creatures
messages in bottles
sailing along
the waters of life
right–side up
at least most of the time
what's up may be down
and what's down may be up
how our eyes look
is how our life develops
keep your eyes on the prize
the most beautiful Divine
speaks to you all the time
in song, verse, and rhyme
in hunches, dreams, and wishes
in visions of higher living
when we lie down at night
our soul takes flight
revealing our subconscious
shown to us so bright
create your reality
lucidly, with faith
may your dreams become real
while you're living and awake

"The dream is the liberation of the spirit from the
pressure of external nature, a detachment of the soul
from the fetters of matter."

– Sigmund Freud

My most inspired dreams become my reality today

Funny

What is funny?
it's not serious
it's funny
like a funny look
or a funny face
with a funny thought
expressed by the funny face
or a funny comment
about something that wasn't funny
but the person made it funny
like a shaman

"Humor is mankind's greatest blessing."

– Mark Twain

I joyously express my sense of humor today

Salt of the Earth

To love and be loved
this is what we need
I grew up in a house
with a yard of apple trees
so sweet
the salt of the earth
can keep a heart warm
let us melt into the sunset
and be the light in early morn

"The living moment is everything."

– D.H. Lawrence

I am energized and uplifted by the beauty of nature today

Lotus–Heart

Floating on the water
remaining untouched
lotus–heart wide open
celebrating love
not too left
not too right
the observant mind
is a beautiful light
not too crazy
not too sane
some madness is beneficial
a little straight, a little gay
do you know what I'm saying?
before you use your eyes
ask what your soul sees
before you have a doubt
trust yourself implicitly

"As soon as you trust yourself, you will know how to
live."

- Johann Wolfgang von Goethe

My unlimited spirit is free from the boxes of identity today

The Healing State

The healing state
is when you go so deep
you forget about your nose,
legs, arms, and feet
it's pure consciousness
it's pure relaxation
your worries unravel
an energetic sublimation
massage, music,
love, compassion
these are great inputs
to cause positive reactions
think beyond yourself
towards what life wants
you can heal others
you're a spiritual savant
by blessing yourself
you bless everyone
by loving yourself
you shine bright like the sun
there's something wondrous
about the higher dimensions
they pull you up
mesmerizing your attention
the healing state
so beautiful to behold
the healing state
a sacred journey to your soul

"Love is the strongest medicine."

– Neem Karoli Baba

I am fully healed and invincibly whole today

Everything to Gain

At the end of the race
struggling to walk
let us remember
the triumph and the love
warrior's heart
philosopher's mind
immortal soul
one with the Divine
the hero's journey
is adventurous and daring
it starts with seeking
it completes by sharing
the path never ends
there is always more
the golden road to Zion
the righteous lion's roar
don't wait until tomorrow
to do the work of today
no time like the present
to make your own way
you have nothing to lose
and everything to gain

"Heroism is the dazzling and glorious concentration of
courage."

– Henri–Frédéric Amiel

I pursue my goals with great courage today

Life Is

Life is waking up
life is song and dance
life is picking your own shoes
shirt, hat, and pants
life is a dream
life is a mystery
life is sacred
you should know your history
life is joy
life is love
life is the sky
life is a dove
life is breath
life is death
life is north, south, east, and west
life is a gift
life is sweet
life never ends
this we'll all see
life is Divine
life is energetic
life is sublime
life is poetic

"A poem is the very image of life expressed in its eternal truth."

– Percy Bysshe Shelley

I let go of control and dive into the miracle of life today

Thank About It

Thankfulness opens the door
for everything brand new
especially the things
that are really good for you
happiness, abundance,
sweetness, serendipity
gratitude gives you
a positive proclivity
to be thankful is
an interesting thing
it humbles the mind
a beautiful surrendering
what we don't have is irrelevant
what we do have is heaven
think about it
be frank about it
be happy every day about it
life is so much better
when thanks is all you say about it

"A thankful heart is not only the greatest virtue, but
the parent of all the other virtues."

– Cicero

I am filled with pure gratitude today

Outside the Lines

A brainy machine
a machine-like brain
are these two different
or exactly the same?
like the zen koan
of one hand clapping
show me the sound
of non-reacting
the Buddha said attachment
is the root of all suffering
outside the lines
is how I do my coloring
you are pure consciousness
in case you start wondering
before the question
beyond the answer
cool like a breeze
graceful like a dancer
what's your beanstalk
if your name was Jack?
today's magic carpet
is a yoga mat
inner peace is a state
without any borders
love is the healing
love is the transformer

"The way is not in the sky. The way is in the heart."

- Buddha

I meditate to discover my inner witness today

God's Eyes

Listen within
for your path to unfold
you're original and unique
soul–expression is the goal
what's inside
is the same for all
pure love of God
and every being, large and small
let your truth live you
set yourself free
we are love's instruments
it's a beautiful reality
let love live you
let your soul see
the Divine intelligence
pervading everything
your light never burns out
your love never dies
the music plays forever
when you're seeing through
God's eyes

"If music be the food of love, play on..."

– William Shakespeare

I am an instrument of spiritual beauty and grace today

Lovers' Walk

As the flower doth
bloom so does love
who will catch
this epic outpouring?
alas, alas
t'is not to be caught
it is to be shared
it is a land
on which lovers walk
without gravity
or shoes

"But how will I know who my soulmate is? By taking risks..."

– Paulo Coelho

I create peace and harmony wherever I go today

A Tree and a Bird

The flowers remind me
of happiness
even though
it is right now happening
happily
a tree and a bird
are always heard
by those in silence
who don't overuse words
beautiful awareness
with what can I compare it
like an open sky, smiling

"The violets in the mountains have broken the rocks."

– Tennessee Williams

I listen to the messages in my life today

Soul Stands Tall

On one level, we age
on another, not at all
the body changes
while the soul stands tall
the spirit of life
never subject to decay
love and devotion
the everlasting way
health is good
laughter is better
it's certainly nice
to have them together
please know this
you've a whole world inside
that never grows old
full of bliss, love and light

"At the height of laughter, the universe is flung into a
kaleidoscope of new possibilities."

– Jean Houston

My presence brings people hope and joy today

A Dream Within a Dream

A dream within a dream
a strange experience indeed
a microcosm of
infinite reality
the still point within
the witness to it all
the atma, the soul
so big and so small
may we all remember
our oneness with the Source
the endless flow of love
the most powerful force
whatever you declare
so it shall be
follow your bliss
a joyous philosophy
the proof in the pudding
the taste in the fruit
now the only time
God the highest truth
tell someone you love them
appreciate them too
embrace your biggest dream
the answer is you

"A dream is a wish your heart makes."

– Walt Disney

I have everything I need to succeed today

Roots and Fruits

The pure food factor
has been proven many times
eat fresh and alive
to supercharge your life
blueberries, blackberries
the Genesis diet
the seed-bearing plants
will keep your doctors quiet
proof of God
in the taste of a mango
look close enough
it's wearing a halo
lose the fat
of the body and mind
cleanse your temple
see through your third eye
sunshine energy
feels so nice
once you jump forward
you'll never look behind
makes your aura glow bright
makes your eyes full of light
the pieces of success
are given to us all
embrace Divine nature
less cooking, more raw

"Food is a love note from God."

– Gabriel Cousens, M.D.

I nourish my body, mind, and soul with positive energy today

Yoga

Yoga is when
gratitude is on your mind
yoga is when
love makes you high
yoga is when
you dance in the rain
yoga is when
you never complain
yoga is when
all is connected
yoga is when
all is perfected
yoga is when
it finally sinks in
yoga is when
your new life begins

"Make yourself so happy so that when others look at
you they become happy too."

– Yogi Bhajan

I am fully present in each moment today

The Greatest Guru

When the ego is gone
no fear remains
when the ego is gone
we all become sane
no need for reaction
no need for hope
all is provided
seeing from your soul
the greatest teachers say
we are here to serve
each and every day
an opportunity to learn
if you play with fire
you're going to get burned
if love is your desire
you're a blessing in the world
the prophets and the saints
they bring us all together
the prophets and the saints
they fly without feathers
if you're so fortunate
to be with a master
your life gets transformed
it's very sought after
the greatest guru
lives in your heart
listen very closely
and you'll go very far

"The best way to find yourself is to lose yourself in the
service of others."

– Mahatma Gandhi

I serve people with unconditional love today

Who is to Say?

What are drugs?
what are emotions?
what are chemicals
in the ocean?
what is serotonin?
what is dopamine?
what is oxytocin?
will we ever get clean?
what is attraction?
what is disdain?
what is ecstasy?
what is pain?
what is happiness?
what is joy?
what is the difference
between a girl and a boy?
beyond the obvious
is not that preposterous
what is sacred?
what is profane?
who has the answers?
who is to say?

"Live your questions now, and perhaps even without knowing it, you will live along some distant day into your answers."

– Rainer Maria Rilke

I ask questions to open my mind to new possibilities today

Do What You Love

Do what you love
the money will follow
life's too short
to feel this hollow
what lights you up?
what makes you excited?
what puts sparkles in your eyes?
what makes your heart delighted?
go do that
and then do it some more
time will freely fly
the best is in store
happiness is
irreplaceable and precious
don't sacrifice it
for a clockwork method
do what you love
that's what life is for
do what you love
and then do it some more

"There is no passion to be found in settling for a life
that is less than the one you are capable of living."

– Nelson Mandela

My passion is the driving force of my life today

Circle of Life

Having children
is such a trip
I remember when
I was just a little kid
playing catch with my Dad
sleepovers with friends
now I am the parent
life's circle never ends

"The soul is healed by being with children."

– Fyodor Dostoyevsky

My inner child is blessed with love today

The Ultimate Goal

Life is so much grander
than the best laid plans
better to place your love in God
than in all the toys of man

"Thou shalt love the Lord thy God with all thy heart,
and with all thy soul, and with all thy mind. This is
the first and great commandment. And the second is
like unto it, thou shalt love thy neighbour as thyself."

– Jesus Christ

I am focused on what truly matters today

This Ancient Beyond

The breath
is anti-death
until the soul waves hello
to a new world
this ancient beyond
is full of super soul-glow
where a smile is everlasting
there is always joyous laughing
and life is how it should be
every now of the now
love is the foundation
of this great nation
of particles and atoms
across all creation
this ancient beyond
is sung with a song
this ancient beyond
is here all along

Namaste: "I honor the place in you, which is of love, of
truth, of light and of peace. When you are in that place
in you, and I am in that place in me, we are one."

The beautiful light of my spirit shines through today

Spin the Bottle

Spin the bottle
on top of a building
kiss the sky
say a prayer with feeling
connect to the effect
of dancing on the ceiling
travel back in time
give the big bang a healing

"Part of the healing process is sharing with other
people who care."

– Jerry Cantrell

I pray for guidance today

Time

What really changes
as time goes by?
how does time fly?
can it kiss the sky?
does it know how to drive?
or is it just
an innocent passerby?
time
the essence of mystery
the container of history
time
if you try to define it
try to outline it
you'll walk right by it
time
a smile and a kiss
a moment of bliss
oh how I love to reminisce
time is the watchdog
time is the healer
time is patience
time is the revealer
down the river we go
praising the most high
the heart, the greatest treasure
love, the greatest why

"Dost thou love life? Then do not squander time, for
that's the stuff life is made of."

– Benjamin Franklin

I utilize every moment wisely today

To Love Someone

To know and to not know
to appreciate the moment
I hear the birds sing
I see the sunshine so golden
this brilliant instant
cannot be saved
people learn things at raves
and dance the night away
to love someone
and forget the rest
to be in that moment
that seems best

"We loved with a love that was more than love."

– Edgar Allan Poe

I move out of my head and into my heart today

Rain Dancer

What comes first
the question or the answer?
if you've got a thirst
become a rain dancer
if you see a problem
be the solution
if something is stuck
be the evolution
life is a journey
life is a flower
each moment is a petal
each feeling is a color
love is the water
the garden is each other

"The more people that meet each other, the better it is
for all of them."

– Giuseppe Mazzini

I focus on win-win solutions today

A Great Chance

Each day, a beautiful day
each breath, a blessing
your soul, your essence
your body, the dressing
each thought, of gratitude
all wishes, for love
deep in your heart
a light like the sun
this is a great chance
to know who we are
this is a beautiful dance
with very beautiful stars
we are here now
and we will always be
soaring in sacred
spiritual eternity
giving love and causing joy
is the enlightened one's routine
aware of and awake to
the Divine reality

"No bird soars too high if he soars with his own wings."

– William Blake

I breathe deeply and mindfully today

Do Something Different

Do something great
go beyond your fear
try something new
what beliefs do you hold dear?
are they helpful, harmful
or somewhere in the middle?
retool the circuitry
like a new tune on your fiddle
identity is
a flexible thing
if you hold on too tight
it can be maddening
the essence of it all
is oneness with life
on this sacred journey
we are all the eyes
of a spiritual presence
like the number eleven
in your heart is heaven
emanating light
climbing so high
do something different
just give it a try

"Things do not change; we change."

– Henry David Thoreau

I see my life with fresh and inspired eyes today

A Sky of Stars

Walking in
the moonlit ocean
feeling how it feels
to be
creating a ripple
of positive energy
what a wonderful sight to see
a sky of stars pulsing quietly
over
a peaceful tree

"Let all your thinks be thanks."

– W.H. Auden

I am in love with the mystery of life today

What If

What if the raindrops stopped
and did a rain dance?
what if the clouds wore shoes
and a pair of sky pants?
what if thoughts of delight
made the light more bright?
what if the trees and the bees
tickled each other's knees?
what if love is life
and life is love?
what if when you look down
it's someone else's above?
what if miracles happen
in the blink of your eyes?
what if the soul lives forever
and only our bodies say goodbye?

"They are ill discoverers that think there is no land,
when they can see nothing but sea."

– Francis Bacon

I connect with the soul of each person I meet today

Love Be Present

A past which goes forever
and a future without end
I am here in this moment
if not now, when?
breathing it all in
with thankfulness and love
this life is very special
I can never get enough
the mystery, the magic
the providential connections
now is the time
live your highest potential
fear be gone
love be present
let's make the whole world
the kingdom of heaven

"Freedom lies in being bold."

– Robert Frost

I make quantum leaps towards my highest potential today

Magnificent Beings

The waves go up
the waves go down
this natural rhythm
is a meditative sound
nature has
a sparkling mystique
nature is
ever-presently unique
what is time
but a mental container?
what is time
is there really a later?
this moment more precious
than all the sky's stars
can we even comprehend it
do we know who we are?
magnificent beings
of natural brilliance
we're all essential parts
of the same amazing sentence
the beginning is the end
and the end is the beginning
your essence is love
love is winning

"Victory belongs to those that believe in it the most
and believe in it the longest."

– Randall Wallace

I clear my mind and open my heart today

The Ultimate Joint Venture

The body is the house
the soul is what's living
love is the answer
love is for giving
feed the children
inspire their hearts
they are the future
they are the stars
let them write the stories
of their original lives
let them see the world
through their innocent eyes
rocketship, spaceship
infinite adventure
two loving parents
the ultimate joint venture
I am in awe
of life itself
the sacred majesty
I can only try to tell
my feelings about it all
I have so much to say
love is the answer
love is the way

"The brightest smiles and bitterest tears spring from
parents' hearts."

– George Seaton Bowes

I share my unique observations with others today

Everyone Lives

Messages from friends
who from this realm are gone
gladden the heart
awaken an old song
everyone lives
no one really dies
this fact is seen
through spiritual eyes
the more love you give
the more love you receive
this remains true
eternally
let us celebrate these days
with friends and family
let us be thankful and rejoice
frequently and happily

"Friendship multiplies the good of life."

– Baltasar Gracian

I give my friends a lot of love today

Break the Dam, Break the Levee

The gifts of life
come in many colors
fall in love with nature
connect to many others
you might be crude
you might be offensive
you might have an attitude
that within you is heaven
you might be funny
you might be rich
you might be tired
you might have an itch
you might be peaceful
you might be grateful
you might be loving
you might be playful
we are all sitting
at the very same table
all are waves
in the ocean of energy
the heart is the river
break the dam, break the levee

"Wheresoever you go, go with all your heart."

– Confucius

I see everyone as a mirror of myself today

Love and Truth

Slow and steady
let's get there already
in front of a million people
creating a million laughs
rebirth is a fantastic sequel
to what you think you don't have
what does it mean
to be in the flow
to radiate happiness
everywhere you go
to not have to think
because of what you know
sharing our gifts
is what we're here to do
a life of enlightenment
is full of love and truth

"There is no joy in possession without sharing."

– Erasmus

I share my talents and gifts with the world today

A New Earth

What once was a secret
is now revealed
what was once a dream
is now so real
what was once fantasy
is now reality
love and enlightenment
is now a widespread mentality
it's a new earth
singing a new song
this is such a great story
in which we all get along
like peas and carrots
cookies and milk
celebrating differences
making love our only will
what was once desired
has now come about
what was once wished for
is happening right now

"Your own self-realization is the greatest service you
can render the world."

– Ramana Maharshi

I am grateful for how far I've come today

Dear Mom

Dear Mom
the light of my life
when I was struggling you cried
that made me feel alive
you're from the Bronx
of course you're wise
Russian roots
a celebratory disposition
thank you Mom
with you I am winning
you love my family
with all your heart
you support everything I do
as if it's the greatest work of art
the greatest fortune
I could ever earn
can never replace
your encouragement I've heard
you are generous, funny
spiritual and full of soul
being with you is a haven
from the world of come and go
you help me see
that life is no accident
you help me feel
pure love to its maximum
Mom you are great
the best, essentially
Mom I'm so grateful for you
joyously, reverentially

"My mother said to me, 'If you are a soldier, you will become a general. If you are a monk, you will become the Pope.' Instead, I was a painter, and became Picasso."

– Pablo Picasso

I feel a sacred and powerful connection to my family today

Dad

Turn back time
by looking at a picture
feel your soul sublime
you know how I've missed you
we used to walk around the block
talking about life
we used to drive in your car
singing voices high
laughing out loud
playing around
in my memories and dreams
can you now be found
what a great dad
what a creative dad
what a fun dad
what a wonderful dad
encouraging me
to be all I can be
championing me
to live confidently
now you must be watching
with a smile so sweetly
you've got grandkids now
and a boy on the way
Dad do you know everything
that is happening today?
your spirit lives
in my very life
we are connected
as the stars are to night
thank you for being
a really great Dad

you supported and consoled me
whenever I was sad
may you always sing
all of your favorite songs
I know you're watching
from the world beyond

"My father gave me the greatest gift anyone could give
another person: he believed in me."

– Jim Valvano

I express thanks to my parents by celebrating my life today

Treat Your Children Well

Treat your children well
time will surely tell
how much love you gave them
how much you made their hearts swell
look into their eyes
speak sweetly with them
they're a very part of you
deeper than you can fathom
evolution of your past
crystals of your future
sometimes your student
sometimes your tutor
like a sacred yin yang
our children light the way
listen to them closely
honor what they say
yes you can
be all you can be
love yourself
connect with God extensively
these are the lessons
to teach them by example
treat your children well
each one a sacred temple

"Live to learn and you will really learn to live."

– John C. Maxwell

I have enlightening conversations with people of all ages today

Love is in the Air

Rainbow cartwheels
sparkling across the sky
magical memories
created tonight
the bliss of a kiss
the sensual surrender
love is in the air
so sweet, so tender
hearts touching
minds melding into one
the rest of our life
has only just begun
tropical rainfall
the mystique, the romance
will you marry me I say
she says yes
we hold hands
the greatest moment
has just occurred
I will be marrying
the most beautiful of girls
a smile that truly
changed my life
her eyes captured me
with a special spark of light
love is more powerful
than all else combined
thank you Pia
for being my wife

"My romance doesn't need a thing but you."

– Ella Fitzgerald

God brings perfect love into my life today

That's Poetry

How high can you jump
without coming down?
be the talk of the town
leap tall buildings
in a single bound
the physics of poetry is
what's thought gets written down
and everything's allowed
black hole revelations
from another time-space continuum
meet your former self
teach him or her some rhythm
let's cross paths
with a groovy kind of love
a Divine dispensation
sweeter than you've ever dreamed of
two step, tango, Irish jig
the words you just read
make you dance in your head
that's poetry, I said

"It is never the thing but the version of the thing."

– Wallace Stevens

I live my life in pure creative freedom today

The Fast Lane

If you look hard enough
you'll find the present moment
after a beautiful day
witness a sunset so golden
here's a promise:
gratitude will change your life
harmonize your frequency
brighten your light
so thankful for
everything and more
gratitude adds
a million points to your score
better to count your blessings
than your supposed misfortunes
it's the fast lane to joy
it's the perfect absorption

"Let gratitude be the pillow upon which you kneel to
say your nightly prayer."

– Maya Angelou

The power of grace flows through my soul today

This Glorious Divinity

This glorious divinity
is beyond the vicinity
of the non-ideal proclivity
to doubt your own ability
to realize the truth
to experience the love
to express your soul
to have peace like a dove
your timeless being
is full of sweet bliss,
immortal inspiration,
and phenomenal genius
go forth and live
go forth and free
yourself and all
from a finite reality
live this life
with heartfelt gusto
live this life
from what your spirit really knows
smile, laugh,
and sing out loud
it's ok to feel happy,
blessed, and proud

"The secret of genius is to carry the spirit of the child
into old age, which means never losing your
enthusiasm."

- Aldous Huxley

My spiritual voice is powerful and amazing today

Diamonds and Rubies

What are we doing?
if we're not growing
what are we doing
if we're not showing
the scars and bruises
from our experience
the wisdom and revelations
from going delirious
life has a way
of being patient with us all
call it grace
call it beautiful
we all climb our own walls
of love, acceptance
and soul-realization
we are born to listen
to our own radio station
turn that dial
to a meditative mind
embrace our struggles
give it all to the Divine
it's all good
it's all great actually
because the scars and bruises
are really diamonds and rubies

"With every adversity comes a blessing."

– Bruce Lee

I use my life experience to help other people today

Conscious Energy

Conscious energy
knows how to flow
conscious energy
like a perfect finger roll
conscious energy
harmony in motion
conscious energy
enjoys love and devotion
conscious energy
is made of bliss
conscious energy
feels like a perfect kiss
conscious energy
is love everyday
conscious energy
is one with the way
conscious energy
knows how to feel
conscious energy
knows what's real
conscious energy
the gift is you
conscious energy
so beautiful, so true

"Follow your bliss and the universe will open doors
where there were only walls."

– Joseph Campbell

I choose everything in my life with spiritual discernment today

Radiance of Spirit

Radiance of spirit
rays of thee sun
ancillary to
the glory of the Lord
syllables like bulls
charging, carrying meaning
to the depth of your being
who creates the created?
something to ponder
ponds and lotuses
birds and bees
just parts of the holy
whole of life
which is a word
commonly used to describe
what is now happening
after we last died
oh glorious everlasting
oh origin of love...

"Better pass boldly into that other world, in the full
glory of some passion, than fade and wither dismally
with age."

– James Joyce

I live in a state of faith and devotion today

Thank You

Thank you to the air
thank you to the trees
thank you to my friends
thank you to my family
thank you to the vegetables
thank you to the fruits
thank you to the old
thank you to the new
thank you to the stars
thank you to the sky
thank you for my soul
thank you for this life
thank you for this breath
thank you for this day
thank you for this moment
thank you in every way
thank you for the past
thank you for the future
thank you for music
thank you for humor
thank you to my arms
thank you to my legs
thank you for my shower
thank you for my bed
thank you for my imagination
thank you for my feelings
thank you for endings
thank you for beginnings
thank you for the losses
thank you for the winnings
thank you for the treat
of making poetry out of living

"When I started counting my blessings, my whole life
turned around."

– Willie Nelson

I am thankful for absolutely everything today

We Are Not Afraid/
Nous Ne Sommes Pas Peur

(reflecting on 11/13/15 terrorist attacks in Paris)

Nous ne sommes pas peur
love is our final word
nous ne sommes pas peur
may love prevail on planet Earth
we are all Paris
we are all implicated
it's OK to feel pain, exasperated
the attackers are attacking
their very own selves
we're part of one body
we're all the living cells
so choose heaven, not hell
beyond forgiveness
beyond blame
at our very core
we are all the same
nous ne sommes pas peur
this life is to cherish
on this night we all
say prayers for Paris

"Compassion is the basis of morality."

– Arthur Schopenhauer

I am the change I wish to see in the world today

This Great Adventure

I left with three duffel bags
put the past behind my back
said goodbye to Mom and Dad
my emotions cracked
shed lots of tears
both happy and sad
I was leaving my home
with my soul blackjack
I took the winding road
across the U.S. of A.
met a lot of different people
along my merry way
healers in New Mexico
friends in California
my sister in Colorado
I even met a woman
who could see my aura
I met a brilliant artist
lived in the middle of the desert
no running water
bore all kinds of weather
he told me he was gay
but he had an older wife
he was the best damn painter
I've ever seen in my life
I met a shaman
who helped me find my new home
first I settled in Santa Fe
then San Diego
the great spirit of life
was truly my guide
for that I am thankful

every day and every night
so much to say
I could go on all day
this trip of mine
this great adventure
is happening right now
and it's never been better

"The biggest adventure you can take is to live the life
of your dreams."

– Oprah Winfrey

I focus on enjoying the journey today

Love All, Serve All

Hare Krishna Hare Krishna
Krishna Krishna Hare Hare
of all sacred mantras
this is my Ferrari
I learned about it
10 years back
I said it, I sang it
put me on the right track
a chance to focus
on what means the most
God, the Source,
the Spirit, the Soul
is not something outside
it's pure love within
makes your mind peaceful
makes your chakras spin
you might even turn
vegetarian
love all, serve all, always remember
that you are certainly
a miraculous conception
the universe is
a sacred soul convention
you are your own ticket
what you pay is your attention

"The miracles of earth are the laws of heaven."

– Jean Paul Richter

I take the high and happy road today

Play Ball

The fine line
between material and Divine
is just an illusion
in your made-up mind
organize yourself
organize your life
take responsibility
make your dreams take flight
the spiritual energy
of love and devotion
is the straight and narrow
in this infinite ocean
a smile develops
gratitude arises
this life is beautiful
like rainbows and sunshine
the universe answers
every soul's call
so pick up the phone
it's time to play ball

"The desire accomplished is sweet to the soul."

- King Solomon

I ask for what I want and I receive it and so much more today

What a Blessing

We are animals with lights on
and doors open wide
to the celestial realm
and even more, the Divine
what a blessing it is
to be alive and free
what a blessing it is
to sing and be happy
what a blessing it is
to smell a sweet lily
what a blessing it is
to be playful and silly
what a blessing it is
to see each other in ourselves
what a blessing it is
to know that all is always well
what a blessing it is
to shine your soul far and wide
what a blessing it is
to see a shooting star at night
what a blessing it is
to speak your truth
oh what a blessing it is
to say I love you

"Sincerity is the way to heaven."

– Mencius

I stop to smell the roses of my life today

The Land of the Free

The land of the free
is this now of eternity
the home of the brave
is this pure love way
amazing grace
such a beautiful place
miraculous conception
spiritual connection
the God–love presence
what really matters
is that you be who you are
what's most important
is that you live from your heart

"There are many paths leading to the top of Mount
Fuji, but there is only one summit – love."

– Morihei Ueshiba

I see the Divine architecture of life today

Divine Union

In the quiet night
of shimmering stars
I want to be
right where you are
Divine union
manifest in our kiss
being in love with you
is the greatest bliss
in the quiet night
during reflection
I thank the Source of life
and to that, our connection
in the quiet night
in the sweet, cool breeze
I am relishing this grace
like a hungry honeybee
on this beautiful night
and forevermore
I love you Pia
it is you who I am for

"Let those love now, who never loved before;
Let those who always loved, now love the more."

- Anonymous (translated by Thomas Parnell, 1722)

I replace fear with love today

Pure Mind

Don't do anything
without your soul
don't say anything
that's less than you know
breathe the open sky
straight to your heart
dance in the sunlight
think love, near and far
if you do one thing
pray everyday
ask for peace, love, happiness
and to be shown the way
if you're going to do another thing
let your light shine
the bliss of the soul
flows through a pure mind
life is love
and you are Divine

"As we let our light shine, we unconsciously give other
people permission to do the same. As we are liberated
from our own fear, our presence actually liberates
others."

– Marianne Williamson

I speak truth to power today

Stay Tuned

Beyond your mind
deeper than your thoughts
the experience of life
can't be sold or bought
life is an adventure
life is more and more love
it's a soul awakening
can be smooth, can be rough
a very great power
is within you
it's a life-changing message
right out of the blue
so be ready, be willing
and most of all
stay tuned

"It is the soul's duty to be loyal to its own desires. It must abandon itself to its master passion."

– Rebecca West

I am available for positive changes in my life today

A Trail of Stars

Physical fitness
of the inner witness
the unconditional lives
on just one condition
keep your mind open
keep your soul free
let God speak to you
let your life be happy
the more you give
the more you believe
the more you give
the more you receive
the more you give
the more you leave
a trail of stars
a trail of jubilation
a trail of love
the angels are waving
the universe is
in constant expansion
let your speech become music
let your steps become dancing

"I would believe only in a God that knows how to
dance."

– Friedrich Nietzsche

I sing and dance in ecstatic joy today

Cosmic Smoothie

I want to rip the stars
from the indifferent sky
and take them as my own
I want to squeeze the morning sun
in my very hands
I will put the stars and the sun
in my blender
the stars are my ice cubes
the afternoon sun is
my beautiful, nourishing orange
and the evening reddish sun
setting so magnificently
this is my apple
in my cosmic smoothie
and the taste
is glorious rushes of glory
forever and ever

"Sunset is the opening music of the night."

– Mehmet Murat Ildan

I am one with the universe and I love it today

Brand New Day

A fractal rainbow
a heart of gold
if you really say so
I'll show you my soul
all linked together
even more, all one
every person is a teacher
every father is a son
your legacy is
what you've created
may not be appreciated
until it's outdated
God loves all
with equal magnificence
loving yourself
is no less significant
the body changes
from youth to old age
the soul jumps forward
to a brand new day
always loves to play
never hesitates what to say
embraces its own way
Divine love on display

"You can discover more about a person in an hour of
play than in a year of conversation."

– Plato

A spirit of play fills my life today

With You I Fly

Sometimes I wake up
feels like I don't have a clue
but I am so happy
because I'm right next to you
your smile is electric
your laughter is my joy
your eyes a magic ocean
the outside world is just noise
when I'm with you
I can't be thankful enough
there's something about you
that is delicate yet tough
a prettiness, a sweetness
an adventurous soul
I want to be with you
wherever I go
we have a family now
isn't that amazing?
blessings incarnate
have I told you lately
there's nothing I'd rather have
than you on my mind
alone I walk
with you I fly

"Love is the condition in which the happiness of
another person is essential to your own."

– Robert Heinlein

I share my heart with my soulmate today

If Time Was a Fantasy

If a day was a night
and a month was a year
if time was a fantasy
if it all became clear
love is the mountaintop
love is the essence
love is the goal
love is the blessing
saying yes to the Divine
is saying yes to your soul
follow your spirit
this is how you grow
into who you really are
into who you're meant to be
be the love, be the change
be the light for all to see

"I am bound to live by the light I have."

– Abraham Lincoln

I free others from suffering today

Each Moment, Each Day

Dreams can be messages
from the great beyond
from your soul
from your heart
like a long-forgotten song
the essence of you
is more than you may know
it's a love, it's a joy
it's a peace, it's a glow
time is ticking
what shall you do?
stay in the darkness
or live your truth?
sacred service to others
can take many forms
a blessing
a meal
even opening a door
we are meant for greatness
in our very own ways
embrace your Divinity
each moment, each day

"Give food to the hungry, water to the thirsty, and
clothes to the naked. Then God will be pleased."

– Sai Baba of Shirdi

I am a blessing to others today

Our Greatest Gifts

Our greatest gifts
are to love and to be
sometimes we don't see
this simplicity

"Simplicity is the ultimate sophistication."

– Leonardo da Vinci

I cleanse and simplify my life today

Philosophy of Jest

Why did I move west
from the original nest?
who needs rest
when you want to be your best?
I used to major
in the philosophy of jest
passed every test
searched for the truth
in everything I said
on a rocket-ship of creativity
I jump out of bed
I'd like a million dollars
multiplied by ten
is that a big blessing
or like kryptonite in lead?
I could handle it no sweat
wouldn't go to my head
people would be clothed
children would be fed
I'd make love and inspiration
abundant and widespread
a magical mindset
is my most liquid asset
what are numbers
but a gamble or a bet
my soul rejoices
at a beautiful sunset
like a poem flowing
towards its beautiful end
only to wake up
and begin anew, again

"To live is to be slowly born."

- Antoine de Saint-Exupéry

My mind is brilliant today

The Realm of the Soul

It is a science
if you can define it
test it, refine it
prove it, describe it
sometimes you must Divine it
if I do this
then this happens
not just once
but an overwhelming fraction
like 80%
or, even higher
50/50 is a coin flip
leaves a lot to be desired
science must be seen
holistically
our thoughts and intentions
exist influentially
the cosmic dance
the yin and yang
Radha and Krishna
all the same
lover and beloved
combining as one
beyond the realm of science
into the realm of the soul
there, there,
there we shall go

"Everything that is in the spiritual world is full of transcendental bliss."

– A.C. Bhaktivedanta Swami

I see how my intentions create my results today

Zen in a Bottle

Green juice
I like mine on the rocks
pour another for me
it's nectar from God
you might laugh now
you might scoff or push back
just drink some already
it's the right type of snack
like a team of superheroes
flying through your veins
kicking the bad stuff out
so you feel great again
green juice is amazing
have some everyday
green juice is so tasty
I'd also like to say
its great for your body
its great for your soul
join the green juice club
if this is new, now you know
green juice is lightning
striking your body with love
it's natural, it's from the planet
you'll love it so much
it's cleansing and energizing
calming for your mind
it's like zen in a bottle
let this poem be your sign
after a few sips
you'll surely get the knack
once you go green
you never go back

"The first wealth is health."

– Ralph Waldo Emerson

I am healthy and strong today

The Most Special Present

Nothing outside
can fulfill what's within
what can never end
can never begin
is life a riddle
or a rhetorical question
or the most special present
just waiting to be opened?
gratitude is the key
unity is the truth
love is the ecstasy
each moment is brand new

"He who is not courageous enough to take risks will
accomplish nothing in life."

– Muhammad Ali

I experience the great treasures of my life today

Atom and Eve

Try to reach
inside the atom
on a warm summer's Eve
try to find the apple
that is completely free

"Meditation utilizes concentration in its highest form."

– Paramahansa Yogananda

Everything I do is filled with my spirituality today

Bright Future

In the very bright future
where the music plays on
these thoughts are the reasons
for all to get along
bathed in light
nourished by love
who breathes is rich
who laughs has won
God is great
the soul is wise
life is a gift
brings tears to your eyes
the blooming flower
the juicy fruit
miracles abound
everywhere you look

"Your life is what your thoughts make it."

– Marcus Aurelius

I am so grateful for each breath I breathe today

Cyclops Vision

Obnoxious dictates
gravitational frustration
untapped lovehate
has checkmate on elation
cyclops vision
sees one in everything
faith is not a bluff
it's a real pair of wings

"When we turn to each other and not on each other,
that's victory. When we build each other and not
destroy each other, that's victory."

– Jesse Jackson

The whole world rises with me as I rise today

About the Author

Jason Rotman is married to the wonderful Pia Rotman and has 3 children: Makale'a, Solana, and Solomon.

Jason graduated with a degree in psychology from Princeton University in 2001.

He is regularly featured on major financial TV media as a financial markets expert. He is co-founder of Valia Capital Management and Lido Isle Advisors.

Jason, with his wife Pia and contributing musicians, released a music album in 2016 called "Divine Devotion" under the group name "Krishna's Kirtan."

He hopes that this book inspires you and brings you to a spiritual and beautiful state of being.

Follow your heart, listen to your intuition, and do what brings you joy!

Thank you for reading!

Contact the author: **jasrotman@gmail.com**

Made in the USA
Middletown, DE
30 October 2017